# Which One?

What can my body do?

Written by Clare Beswick and Sally Featherstone

Illustrated by Martha Hardy

A Little Baby Book
Published by Featherstone Education

Featherstone Education

## Key to stages of development

Heads up lookers and communicators

Sitters, standers and explorers

Movers, shakers and players

Walkers, talkers and pretenders

# About Little Baby Books

'Birth to Three Matters' (DfES SureStart 2002), the framework for effective practice with babies and very young children, sends a clear unequivocal message underlining the importance of home and family working together with practitioners to lay the best possible foundations for life and learning. It is a recognition and celebration of the individuality of babies and young children. It provides a wealth of guidance and support to those with responsibility for their care and education.

The Little Baby Book series builds on the principles of the guidance and provides practical handbooks, with a wealth of easy to follow ideas and activities for babies and young children from birth to three.

The Birth to Three framework identifies four aspects which highlight the skills and competence of babies and young children as well as showing the link between growth, learning, development and the environment in which they are cared for and educated.

These four aspects of the Framework are:
* A strong child (Purple Books)
* A skilful communicator (Pink Books)
* A competent learner (Green Books)
* A healthy child (Blue Books)

All the activities use objects and resources readily available in homes and settings. They allow babies and children to develop at their own pace, to make unhurried discoveries and allow for much repetition as well as trying out of new ideas. It encourages children to become increasingly independent, making their own choices. All the activities require the careful and skilful support of an adult. The role of the adult is included in the step-by-step 'What you do' section.

# Which One?

What can my body do?

## About 'Which One?'

**Which One?** is part of the Little Baby Books series and focuses on the aspect– A Healthy Child.

Within this aspect there are four components:
* Emotional well being
* Growing and developing
* Keeping safe
* Healthy choices

Healthy choices, the focus of this Little Baby Book, is about babies and young children discovering and learning about their bodies, making choices and expressing their individual preferences, making decisions and becoming aware of others and their needs.

All the activities in this book aim to enable babies and young children to:
* become confident.
* develop trust.
* make genuine choices.
* develop awareness of their own needs.
* become aware of the needs of others.
* develop early interaction skills.
* take turns.
* develop language skills.
* have a sense of shared fun.
* explore their bodies.
* imitate actions.
* try new ways of moving.
* use two hands together effectively.
* find out about fingers and thumbs!
* explore and discover.
* harness a sense of curiosity.
* encounter genuine praise.

Your role as practitioner or parent will be varied and will include:
* Facilitating
* Observing
* Prompting
* Negotiating
* Leading
* Imitating
* Focusing

## Which One?

What can my body do?

**Aspect:**
A healthy child
**Components:**
making healthy choices

# Why are these activities so important?

Babies and children need to feel safe and secure. Learning, growing and independence must be grounded in a secure sense of being supported and valued, particularly by key care-givers.

Babies feel secure when:
- they are held and cuddled.
- they have eye contact with others.
- they feel warm and protected.
- they can stretch out their hands, arms, feet and legs without feeling exposed.
- they see smiles and interest in their care-givers' faces.

Older children feel secure when:
- they know what is going to happen to them.
- they have clear rules and boundaries.
- they can play freely without fear of danger.
- they can take reasonable risks in activities without fear of failure.
- they have familiar friends and adults around them.
- people are interested in them, their unique needs and strengths.
- their successes are celebrated.
- they have high self esteem and confidence.

And of course, babies and children develop more quickly if they have the support and company of gentle, loving adults who know them well and get involved in their play. The encouragement, language, example and inspiration of the caring adult is vital to children's growth. They need you with them, helping them to explore and make sense of the world from a secure base.

# Watch, listen, reflect

Assessing babies' and children's learning is a difficult process, but we do know that any assessment must be based on careful observation of children in action.

On each activity page, you will see a box labelled **Watch, listen, reflect.** This box contains suggestions of what you might look and listen for as you work and play with the babies and children. Much of the time you will watch, listen and <u>remember</u>, using your knowledge of early years and of the children and reflecting on the progress of the individual child. These informal observations will help you to plan the next day's or week's activities.

However, sometimes what you see is new evidence. Something you have never seen the child do before, or something which concerns you. In these cases you might make a written note of the achievement you see, and the date and time you observed it. You will use these notes for a range different purposes, and some of these are:

- 👁 to remind you of the event or achievement (it's easy to forget in a busy setting!).
- 👁 to use in discussion with your manager or other practitioners.
- 👁 to contribute to the child's profile or record.
- 👁 to discuss with parents.
- 👁 to help with identifying or supporting additional needs.
- 👁 to help with planning for individuals.
- 👁 to make sure you tell everyone about the child's achievements.

Observation is a crucial part of the complex job you do, and time spent observing and listening to children is never wasted.

# Which One?

What can my body do?

**Aspect:**
A healthy child
**Components:**
making healthy choices

## Which One?

What can my body do?

# Keeping safe

Safety must be the top priority when working with any baby or young child, at nursery or at home. All the activities in Little Baby Books are suitable for under threes. You will already have a health and safety policy but here are just a few top tips for safe playing with babies and young children.

**Watch for choking hazards.**
Young babies and children naturally explore toys by bringing them to their mouths. This is fine, but always check that toys are clean. If you are concerned, buy a choke measure from a high street baby shop.

**Never leave babies or young children unattended**
They are naturally inquisitive and this needs to be encouraged, BUT they need you to watch out for them. Make sure you are always there.

**Check for sharp edges.**
Some everyday objects or wooden toys can splinter. Check all toys and equipment regularly. Don't leave this to chance – make a rota.

**Ribbons and string.**
Mobiles and toys tied to baby gyms are a great way to encourage looking and reaching, but do check regularly that they are fastened securely. Ribbons and string are fascinating for babies and children of all ages – but they can be a choking hazard.

**Clean spaces.**
Babies are natural explorers. They need clean floors. Store outdoor shoes away from the under threes area.

**Sitters and standers.**
Make sure of a soft landing for babies and young children just getting there with sitting and standing balance. Put a pillow behind babies who are just starting to sit. Keep the area clear of hard objects, such as wooden bricks. Look out for trip hazards for crawlers and walkers.

**High and low chairs.**
Make sure babies and young children are fastened securely into high chairs and that chairs are moved out of the way when not in use. Use a low chair and table for young children. Try to make a foot-rest if their feet don't reach the ground. Watch out for chairs that tip easily.

# Contents

| | | |
|---|---|---|
| About Little Baby Books | page | 2 |
| Introduction to this book | pages | 3 and 4 |
| Observing and assessing learning | page | 5 |
| Keeping safe | page | 6 |
| Happy hands! - hands together and to face | pages | 8 and 9 |
| Look and pat - black and white pat mats | pages | 10 and 11 |
| Blanket rockers - making first choices | pages | 12 and 13 |
| Splash or drizzle? - more choices, a water play game | pages | 14 and 15 |
| Bend and stretch - copying actions | pages | 16 and 17 |
| In the box - choosing which song | pages | 18 and 19 |
| Terrific textures - treasure basket of textures | pages | 20 and 21 |
| Heavenly hats - reaching, stretching, stopping, starting! | pages | 22 and 23 |
| In we go! - still more choices | pages | 24 and 25 |
| Truly sloppy! - cornflour and water play | pages | 26 and 27 |
| Teddy and Co - what's for dinner? | pages | 28 and 29 |
| Drink time! - still more choices! | pages | 30 and 31 |
| All wrapped up - twisting, wrapping, folding | pages | 32 and 33 |
| Baby time! - baby play with everyday objects | pages | 34 and 35 |
| Music makers - making choices with improvised instruments | pages | 36 and 37 |
| Look at me! - exploring movement | pages | 38 and 39 |
| Special – it's mine - choosing favourites | pages | 40 and 41 |
| I like…. - books and stories | pages | 42 and 43 |
| Resources | page | 44 and 45 |
| Information about the series | page | 46 |

# Which One?

What can my body do?

**Aspect:**
A healthy child
**Components:**
making healthy choices

## Which One?

What can my body do?

**Heads up lookers and communicators**

**Aspect:**
A healthy child
**Components:**
making healthy choices

# Happy hands – hands together and to face

## What you need
* wrist toy or elastic hair scrunchie

## What you do

1. Sit opposite the baby or with the baby on your knee. Lie young babies on their back on a soft rug. Place a rolled up blanket either side of wrigglers – so they can focus on their hands rather than their escape!
2. Gently bring the babies hands together in the midline and sing, using a tune you are comfortable with:
    *Happy hands, happy hands*
    *Touch it, feel it, happy hands*
3. Tap the baby's hands together gently. Encourage them to feel and shake the wrist toy. Give them plenty of time for unhurried and uninterrupted exploration.
4. Sing the song again, and this time gently help the child bring their hands together in the midline and then up to their face so that they can gaze at their hands.

## Ready for more?

- Play the game with a wrist toy or bells on their ankle. Sing 'Happy Feet'.
- Play lots of clapping games to encourage older babies to bring two hands together in the mid-line.

## Individual needs

☼ Vary the pace or use funny voices and whispers to grab their attention.
☼ Securely attach bells to wrist toys for babies and children that need an extra reward.
☼ Look out for black and white wrist toys for added appeal.

## Tiny Tip

✻ Wrist toys are a great way to encourage young babies to lie still at changing time!

## Watch, listen, reflect

👁 Think about the different ways the baby is exploring the wrist toy.
👁 Watch to see if they spontaneously bring their hands towards their face.
👁 Listen to the sounds they make. How is the baby using sounds or body language to communicate?

## Working together

### Parents could:

* try the 'Happy hands' song at home with their baby, perhaps as part of getting dressed, when they have put their baby's arms in sleeves and so on.
* Play 'Pat a Cake' with their baby.

### Practitioners could:

* make sure the words and actions of the happy hands song are available to parents.
* share with parents the importance of finger play and discovery.

## Which One?

What can my body do?

### What are they learning?

are they
  exploring?
  looking for the sound?
  enjoying rhymes?
  bringing hands together?
this leads to
  * clapping
  * patting
  * reaching

## Which One?

What can my body do?

**Heads up lookers and communicators**

**Aspect:**
A healthy child
**Components:**
making healthy choices

# Look and pat –
### black and white pat mats

## What you need
* black and white fabric
* stick-on Velcro or a simple sewing kit
* scraps of crunchy or crinkly paper for filling

## What you do
1. Make a simple bag using the Velcro or straight seams for the edges. Fill the bag with scraps of crunchy or crinkly paper. Seal it securely with Velcro or stitching.
2. Place the mat on a flat surface and encourage the baby to pat the mat using two hands together. Talk and sing as the baby pats the mat.
3. Copy the baby's actions and sing 'Pat, pat, pat'. Vary your voice to grab the baby's attention.
4. Try big slow movements and then quick tiny pats.

**another idea:**
* Fill the bag with soft sponge or feathers. Add some squeakers for added appeal.

## Ready for more?
- Try patting the mat with alternate hands.
- Make a giant stamping mat with just a little filling for older or more mobile babies.
- Can older babies isolate their index finger and poke the mat?

## Individual needs

☼ Add noisy toys, bells and squeakers to for children with hearing impairment.
☼ Move the mat to different positions for babies and children with motor difficulties, to find the best place.
☼ Tickle backs of hands of babies with fisted hands to uncurl their fingers and pat with a flat open hand.

## Tiny Tip

✤ White fabric paint on plain black fabric is a quick and easy way to transform inexpensive fabric.

## Watch, listen, reflect

👁 Look to see how the child is reaching, patting and grasping.
👁 Watch and listen for how they are enjoying this play. How are they letting you know how they feel.
👁 Think about which part of the activity is most rewarding for the child and work out how you know this.

## Working together

### Parents could:
* put small toys on a tray for the baby to pat and explore.
* give their baby damp sponges and flannels to pat at bath time
* try the local toy library for black and white toys, pictures and patterns for their baby.

### Practitioners could:
* ask parents to bring in scraps of black and white fabric and clothes.
* talk to parents about the appeal of black and white patterns to babies.
* place a black and white mobile over the changing area.

## Which One?

What can my body do?

### What are they learning?

are they
  reaching?
  copying?
  looking?
  using two hands together?
this leads to
  * exploring
  * finding out about bodies
  * clapping

## Which One?

What can my body do?

Heads up lookers and communicators

**Aspect:**
A healthy child
**Components:**
making healthy choices

# Blanket rockers - making first choices

## What you need
* a strong, soft blanket
* a soft mat, rug or mattress
* a helper

## What you do

1. Fold the blanket in half for extra strength and lay it on the mat. Place the baby gently on the blanket, gather up two corners each to make a high-sided hammock.
2. Gently lift the baby in the blanket. With a soft and gentle rhythm and rocking action, sing and rock the baby,
   > Rocking, rocking, to and fro,
   > This is the way we go
   > Rocking, rocking, to and fro,
   > This is the way we stop
   
   Gently bring the blanket back down onto the mat.
3. Watch to see if the baby has enjoyed the activity. Offer 'Again?' Wait for some indication, a glance, a kick, a bounce, or maybe a sound to tell you that the song and rocking should be repeated.

## Ready for more?

- Sing a bouncing rhyme, gently jigging the blanket up and down.
- Try 'Row the Boat' and other rocking songs.
- Add 'Ready steady go', with a pause before 'Go', before each song or game.

## Individual needs

✿ Some children with special needs find rocking very comforting and this can get in the way of them trying other things. For these children use the activity as a reward.
✿ Give lots of verbal reassurance and touches to children needing more reassurance.

## Tiny Tip

✽ Roll in the sides of a small parachute to make a strong hammock for this game.

## Watch, listen, reflect

👁 Look for anticipation of the song.
👁 Watch and listen to see how the child is communicating their feelings about the activity.
👁 See how they are balancing in the blanket. Are they confidently using their hands for support?
👁 Think about the different ways they are letting you know what they want.

## Working together

### Parents could:

* sing the rhyme as they hold their child close and rock from foot to foot.
* think about how their baby lets them know what they want.
* spend a few minutes every day to sing a few simple rhymes with their child.

### Practitioners could:

* make sure there are plenty of song and rhyme books available for parents to look at
* tell parents how their child enjoyed the activity and how they 'asked' for more.

## Which One?

What can my body do?

### What are they learning?

are they
　enjoying new movements?
　asking for more?
　sharing fun?
this leads to
　* confidence with movement
　* finding out about bodies
　* making choices

# Which One?

What can my body do?

**Sitters, standers and explorers**

**Aspect:**
A healthy child
**Components:**
making healthy choices

## Splash or drizzle? – first choices

### What you need
* a small sponge
* a flannel or cloth
* warm water
* small shallow tray such as an ice cream tub

### What you do

1. Place just a few cm of warm water in the tray. Give the baby the dry sponge to feel. Encourage them to use two hands to reach, pat, grasp and squeeze the sponge.
2. Drop the sponge in the warm water. Play at squeezing the warm water over baby's fingers.
3. Give them the dry flannel. Scrunch it up in a ball and encourage them to poke, prod and squeeze it. Drop it into the warm water.
4. After a moment, take the flannel back, dip in the water and then offer a choice. Say 'Which one?' holding up the flannel and the sponge and encouraging the child to look, point, reach for or ask for the item they want.
6. Continue playing offering choices and having fun splashing and drizzling the water.

### Ready for more?

- Use a tin lid or metal tray. The water will make a great sound as it hits the metal!
- Have wet cloths and sponges in a bucket for the child to wring out. Encourage them to ask for and choose from the bucket.

## Individual needs

- Make sure babies and children with motor difficulties are sitting well supported.
- Look out for different sizes and shapes of sponges for children with fine motor difficulties.
- Try lots of different textured sponges and flannels with favourite characters.

## Tiny Tip

Washing up sponges with long handles are a great way to practice reaching and grasping, and wet, are ideal for early mark making.

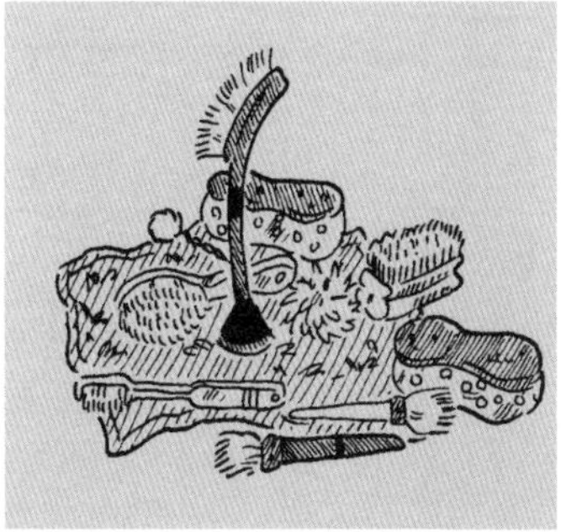

## Watch, listen, reflect

- Observe all the different ways the child is exploring the objects.
- Watch to see how they use their hands together, isolate index fingers for prodding, and the different grips they use to grasp the sponges and flannels.
- Think about all the different ways they are letting you know their choices.

## Working together

### Parents could:

* play this activity at bath time.
* try some simple pretend play with their child, such as brushing hair, wiping faces and so on.
* offer real choices whenever practical, such as 'Do you want milk or water?'.

### Practitioners could:

* build choices into every-day routines - such as 'Should we wash your hands or your face first?' and so on.
* talk to parents about all the different ways babies and young children communicate before words.

## Which One?

What can my body do?

### What are they learning?

are they
- making choices?
- reaching and grasping?
- asking for more?
- sharing fun?
- grabbing/holding?

this leads to
- * confidence
- * making choices
- * independence

## Which One?
What can my body do?

**Sitters, standers and explorers**

**Aspect:**
A healthy child
**Components:**
making healthy choices

# Bend and stretch –
## copying actions

### What you need
* a quiet space
* lots of energy!
* just two or three children

### What you do
1. Start jumping up and down and encourage the children to join you. Try jumping together holding hands.
2. When everyone is sitting, stretch out your legs and tap you toes gently on the floor, and sing 'Stretch, stretch, stretch just like me, I'm as busy as a bumble bee'.
3. Next lie down and stretch out your arms over your head and sing 'Stretch, stretch stretch, stretch like me, I'm as tall, as a tall, tall tree'. Sit up and play the game again.
4. Now, stand up together, and when everyone is ready first bend down low and sing, in a deep voice,
   *Bend, bend, bend, getting very very small,*
   *Stretch, stretch, stretch, getting very very tall*
   *Bend, stretch, bend, stretch, busy as a bee*
   *And now, my hands are on my knee!*

### Ready for more?
- Copy a child's actions, such as patting or clapping, singing a song to describe the actions, such as 'patting, patting just like *name*'.
- Practice getting in and out of large cardboard boxes.

## Individual needs

- ✺ Play this game with just one child, for children with attention or social interaction difficulties.
- ✺ For young children with autistic spectrum disorders, start by imitating the child's actions and singing a commentary.
- ✺ Try silly voices and different rhythms to grab their attention.

## Tiny Tip

❊ Remove as many distractions as possible and vary the pace of action rhymes to keep children interested.

## Watch, listen, reflect

- 👁 Note what grabs the attention of the children.
- 👁 Watch to see if the children can copy the actions and sustain their attention.
- 👁 Think about which tunes and rhythms are most appealing to the children and try to work out why.
- 👁 Watch how the children relate to each other during this activity.

## Working together

### Parents could:
- ★ sing simple commentaries to their child.
- ★ encourage the child to join in everyday tasks at home and copy actions such as dusting, brushing, wiping and so on.

### Practitioners could:
- ★ make time for action rhymes, individually and in small groups, every day.
- ★ encourage children to get involved in tasks around the setting.

## Which One?

What can my body do?

### What are they learning?

are they
   imitating actions?
   learning how their body moves?

this leads to
   * confidence
   * being part of a small group
   * Attention and listening skills

## Which One?

What can my body do?

**Sitters, standers and explorers**

**Aspect:**
A healthy child
**Components:**
making healthy choices

# In the box –
## choosing which song

### What you need
* a high sided cardboard box
* a small cushion

### What you do
1. Help the child to climb into the box and sit on the cushion.
2. Tip the box gently from side to side as you sing "Bobby Shaftoe's gone to sea, silver buckles on his knee, he'll come back and marry me, bonny Bobby Shaftoe'.
3. Ask the child 'Again?'. Wait for a response, looking for non-verbal signals such as a glance or body language, as well as listening for sounds, and then repeat the game.
4. Next, jiggle the front of the box up and down to the rhyme 'Horsey, horsey, don't you stop, just let your hooves go clippity clop'.
5. Jiggle the front of the box and ask 'Horsey Horsey', or 'Bobby Shaftoe' (tipping the box from side to side). Pause to allow the child to think and make their choice. As soon as they let you know, sing that song again.

### Ready for more?
- Do an inset puzzle together, each time asking the child to choose between two pieces, and giving them that piece to replace.
- Play a throwing game, with the child choosing from a box of balls.

## Individual needs

✿ Encourage children to use a pointing gesture, a touch pointing gesture or reach to indicate a choice in young children with communication difficulties.
✿ Start by making choices between two real familiar objects.
✿ Allow plenty of uninterrupted time for the child to process the information.

## Tiny Tip

✽ Be mindful that some children may not be making real choices, but just repeating the last thing offered!

## Watch, listen, reflect

👁 Watch carefully for non-verbal signals, body language, eye pointing.
👁 Listen for the child anticipating key phrases or actions during the rhyme.
👁 Think about their choices and what they are enjoying.
👁 Look at how they are balancing and moving with the movement of the box.

## Working together

### Parents could:

* keep a large cardboard box for the child to enjoy.
* offer real choices, such as which cup would you like, the red one or the blue one.

### Practitioners could:

* build choices into everyday routines.
* put up a list of all the different ways choices are offered to children in your group, and make some suggestions for choices that could be offered at home.

## Which One?

What can my body do?

### What are they learning?

are they
  making choices?
  combining words and gestures?
  sharing fun?
  trying something new?
this leads to
  * sharing
  * making choices
  * joining in

# Which One?

What can my body do?

**Sitters, standers and explorers**

**Aspect:**
A healthy child
**Components:**
making healthy choices

# Terrific treasures – a treasure basket of textures

## What you need
* a shallow basket or container
* everyday objects of different textures - sponges, brushes, metal and wooden spoons, pans, tin lids, plugs and chains, pegs etc

## What you do
1. Sit on the floor with the child and encourage them to explore the treasure basket.
2. Copy their actions with each object, helping them to feel, rub, pat, smell the object on different parts of their body.
3. Talk and sing about the objects and demonstrate their use, such as stirring with the spoon and so on.
4. Encourage them to poke their fingers into holes, peek through objects and so on. Tap and rub the objects on each other.

**another idea:**
* Play at emptying and refilling the basket.

## Ready for more?
- Make collections of everyday objects around a theme, such as getting dressed or dinner time.
- Glue some lengths of cord or ribbon to card. Practice isolating index fingers and following the textured trails.

## Individual needs

☼ Try exploring just a few very familiar objects with children at an early developmental stage.
☼ Look out for brightly coloured or fluorescent coloured objects for children with visual impairment.
☼ Allow plenty of time for exploration and repetition.

## Tiny Tip

❋ Treasure baskets are great things to have to hand at the start of a busy day. Collect plenty of different baskets so babies can have one each.

## Watch, listen, reflect

◉ Look at how the children are exploring the objects and the skills and senses they are using.
◉ Note whether they understand the use of the objects and recognise the names.
◉ Look to see if they bring objects together, such as put the spoon in the pan and so on.
◉ Listen for attempts at first words.

## Working together

### Parents could:

* put together a treasure basket of everyday objects for the child to explore.
* bring in objects with interesting textures for the group.

### Practitioners could:

* put up a list of interesting objects for a treasure basket.
* build collections for treasure baskets, encouraging exploring and 'in and out' play.

## Which One?

What can my body do?

### What are they learning?

are they
  exploring texture?
  using senses?
  learning names and use of objects?
  grabbing/holding?
this leads to
  * sensory play
  * pretend play
  * naming

## Which One?

What can my body do?

**Movers, shakers and players**

**Aspect:** A healthy child
**Components:** making healthy choices

# Heavenly hats –
reaching, stretching, stopping, starting

## What you need
* a collection of different hats – helmets, sun hats, rain hats, woolly hats, straw hats, caps
* a wall mirror, at an easily accessible height
* a tape or CD of dance music

## What you do
Three children is about right for this activity.
1. Spread the hats out on the floor and give the children plenty of time to explore them, trying them on themselves and on you.
2. Place all the hats on the floor and get the children to stand around the edge.
3. Play the dance music. Dance together. When the music stops, each child chooses a hat.
4. Start the music again, dance and when the music stops, swap for a different hat!

**another idea:**
* Pass the hat around the group and when the music stops the child holding the hat puts it on. Choose another hat and play again. Keep going until all the children have a hat.

### Ready for more?
- Wear hats and dance to music. When the music stops, nod the hat off! When it starts again, everyone grabs a hat and starts dancing again!
- See how many hats you can balance on your head and walk from one end of the room to the other!

## Individual needs

✿ Make sure the hats are easy to pull on and off, floppy sun hats work well.
✿ Help easily excited children know the game is over, by taking turns to toss hats back into a box.
✿ Leave some hats in the home corner for shy children to try when they are ready.

## Tiny Tip

❋ Charity shops have some great inexpensive hats, scarves and gloves at bargain prices! Try 'pound shops' for baseball caps and sun hats.

## Watch, listen, reflect

◉ Look to see if children are watching each other.
◉ Watch to see if any of the children are anticipating you turning off the music.
◉ See how quickly the children pick up the rules of this simple game.
◉ Are the children making choices about which hat they want? Are they aware of the needs of others?

## Working together

### Parents could:

* dance with their child!
* ask amongst friends and family for old hats for your group.

### Practitioners could:

* make sure children can reach CDs and tapes, so they can ask for music to be played.
* check that the dressing up clothes are attractive and in good repair.
* fix a full-length mirror at child height.

## Which One?

What can my body do?

### What are they learning?

are they
    moving with confidence?
    listening?
    making choices?
    being part of a group?
this leads to
    * group play
    * listening skills
    * following rules

# Which One?

What can my body do?

**Movers, shakers and players**

**Aspect:**
A healthy child
**Components:**
making healthy choices

# In we go! – still more choices

## What you need
* a tunnel or indoor play tent
* old curtains or blankets
* net curtains or similar fabric
* a large cardboard box
* some soft toys

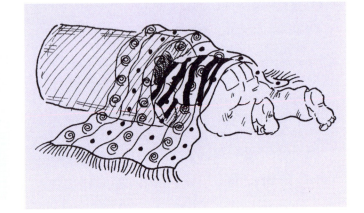

## What you do
1. Open out the cardboard box at both ends to form a short tunnel. Cover the entrances of the box and the tunnel or indoor play tent with the old blankets, curtains or nets.
2. Ask the children to hide the soft toys in the tents.
3. Now play at finding different toys. Give the children plenty of choices, such as 'Should we find Teddy or Rabbit?'.
4. Be explorers and choose different entrances to the tunnels and tent.

another idea:
* Add some torches to take into the tunnels and tents.

## Ready for more?
- Make some holes in the sides of the box for peeking in, or shining torches through.
- Fix some pictures or photos to the insides of the box, tunnel and play tent. Ask the children to hunt for named pictures.

## Individual needs

☼ Make sure the tunnels and tents are on a soft surface suitable for children who are crawling or rolling.
☼ Use a transparent tunnel and net curtain for children needing more reassurance.
☼ Use just the play tent and offer just two choices for children at an early developmental stage.

## Tiny Tip

✻ Take every opportunity to try out different ways of moving – giant strides to the milk table, slithering over to the coats and so on.

## Watch, listen, reflect

👁 Look out for turn taking.
👁 Watch to see how children are relating to each other and for awareness of the needs of others.
👁 Think about the choices each child is making and why.
👁 Listen for action words as well as object words.

## Working together

### Parents could:

* encourage their child to try out different ways of moving.
* provide blankets and boxes for simple den building.

### Practitioners could:

* think of all ways children can move and provide opportunities for children to experiment with movement.
* display information on local facilities for play and lists of local parks on the parent's notice board.

## Which One?

### What are they learning?

are they
   moving with confidence?
   exploring?
   making choices?
   taking turns?
this leads to
   * group play
   * sharing and working together

25

## Which One?

What can my body do?

**Movers, shakers and players**

**Aspect:**
A healthy child
**Components:**
making healthy choices

# Truly sloppy! – cornflour and water play

## What you need
* aprons!
* plastic bowls, jugs, wooden spoons
* plastic scrapers, tubes and tea strainers
* large shallow plastic tray

## What you do

Children will need protective clothing for this activity, which support decision making and choice.
1. Cover everything and the children well!
2. Tip cornflour into the bowls and slowly add water.
3. Mix together using hands or wooden spoons.
4. Play with the cornflour mixture, tipping it into the shallow tray. Encourage the children to isolate their index finger to drizzle the mixture around, use two hands together to hold the bowls and stir, two hands together to pour and steady the jugs.
5. Rub sticky fingers together. Try rubbing the mixture in the flat of open palms, or between fingers and thumbs.

**another idea**:
* Add split peas or uncooked rice to the mixture.

## Ready for more?

👋 Try mark making with fingers in a cornflour and water paste. Add brushes, corks, straws and rollers for more mark making in the goo.

👋 Coloured rice or split peas are great fun with tiny spoons and ice cube trays.

## Individual needs

☼ Some children may dislike the feel of the cornflour and water mixture. Make sure you have lots of clean handled tools for them to use and a clean apron too!
☼ Encourage reluctant children to get involved by adding treasure to the mix – such as sequins or large buttons.
☼ Be aware of allergies and skin irritation.

## Tiny Tip

✲ Tiny containers and spoons fascinate young children. Ice cube trays, clean fromage frais pots and tiny Tupperware containers are ideal.

## Watch, listen, reflect

👁 Watch for children isolating their index finger, using a pincer grip and so on. Can they use two hands together effectively?
👁 Listen for action words and describing words, and short phrases combining action and object words.
👁 Look to see how the children are trying out their own ideas, as well as copying the actions of others.

## Working together

### Parents could:

* give their child a small bowl of jelly to play with!
* make sure that their child has lots of opportunity to try mark making.

### Practitioners could:

* make a recipe poster with play ideas – perhaps a simple play dough recipe, cornflour and water and so on.
* update the range of tools available for the children to use with malleable materials.

## Which One?

What can my body do?

### What are they learning?

are they
　practising hand-eye co-ordination and different grips?
　using two hands together?
　trying new things?
this leads to
　* sensory play
　* motor control

## Which One?

What can my body do?

Movers, shakers and players

**Aspect:**
A healthy child
**Components:**
making healthy choices

# Teddy and company – what's for dinner?

## What you need
* teddies and other soft toys
* small plastic bowls, spoons
* dried pasta, some pretend fruit and some pretend food such as sausages or pizza
* two small chairs or cushions

## What you do
1. Sit a couple of soft toys on the chairs or cushions. Explain that they are really hungry. Rub their tummies and say 'Look, Teddy's feeling hungry'.
2. Invite each child to choose pasta or fruit for Teddy. Help them to fill a bowl and pretend to feed Teddy.
3. Play again, feeding the other toys. Use action words, object words and short phrases. Emphasise key words and phrases, such as 'all gone', 'hungry' and 'full'.
4. Talk to the children about mealtimes at home and in your setting. Ask about favourite foods.

**another idea:**
* Play this simple choice making game with soft toy animals, with clean pet food boxes, an empty milk carton to give the cat a drink, pretend lettuce and carrots for rabbits.

## Ready for more?
- Pass a box of play jewellery around a group of three children, taking turns to choose an item to put on. Pass a mirror round so each child can see how they look.
- Make lots of different coloured paper planes. Take turns to choose a paper plane and fly it.

## Individual needs

☼ Offer real choices between two familiar everyday objects to children with language delay.
☼ Give children with sensory difficulties plenty of time to explore the choices.
☼ Use visual clues such as objects, photos, or line drawings, as well as gestures to support understanding of choices.

## Tiny Tip

✼ Take photos of every-day objects around your setting. Use the photos to support understanding and choice, and as visual clues.

## Watch, listen, reflect

👁 Listen to how children express their choices. Are they aware of others, allowing time for them to make their choice?
👁 Note whether they making genuine choices, or following other children or yourself?
👁 Watch to see if the children can take turns and maintain their attention when it is another's turn.

## Working together

### Parents could:

* offer real choices to their child at every opportunity.
* talk to their child as they are making their own choices.

### Practitioners could:

* talk to parents about the importance of children making choices.
* look at drink and mealtime routines and consider how choice making can be extended for children at every stage.

## Which One?

What can my body do?

### What are they learning?

are they
  making choices?
  expressing their needs?
  using first words to describe feelings?
  taking turns?
this leads to
  * turn taking
  * following rules

# Which One?

What can my body do?

**Walkers, talkers and pretenders**

**Aspect:**
A healthy child
**Components:**
making healthy choices

# Drink time! – still more choices

## What you need
* ice cube trays
* jug of chilled water
* selection of fruit juices
* large tea- or dessert spoons
* small jugs or beakers
* access to a freezer or freezer compartment in a fridge

## What you do
1. Help the children to choose different fruit juices for each compartment of the ice cube trays.
2. Pour small quantities of juice into the small jugs and encourage the children to add other juices to make fruit cocktail mixtures.
3. Encourage the children to stir the mixtures well and then spoon some into each compartment of the ice cube trays.
4. Top up with the chilled water and freeze thoroughly.
5. At drinks time, help each child to pour a small beaker of water and then to add some of the frozen fruit juice ice cubes to their drinks with a spoon.
6. Focus on making choices, and using words and phrases to describe how the juice ice cubes taste. Model simple choices, such as 'Would you like this….or this…..?'.

## Ready for more?
- Encourage children to take turns to offer choices to other children or adults.
- Encourage children to look at lots of books, before choosing a book for you to share with the children.

## Individual needs

☼ Some children may be sensitive to or dislike cold or fruity drinks. Adapt the activity to include known preferences.

☼ Give children plenty of opportunity to try different tastes, experience different flavours and the aromas of a wide range of different foodstuffs.

## Tiny Tip

❋ Make tasting and exploring new foods a part of every theme or topic.

## Watch, listen, reflect

👁 Look to see how children manipulate the jug, spoon and so on. Are they using two hands together?

👁 Listen to the words and phrases children use to label and describe.

👁 Watch how they explore the materials used in this activity.

👁 Watch to see how confident the children are to try new experiences and how you can encourage them.

## Working together

### Parents could:

* encourage their child to explore the texture and smell of different foodstuffs.
* let their child choose the bedtime story book.

### Practitioners could:

* make a list of some of the choices that could be offered at home and in the setting. Put this up where everyone can see it.
* include a statement about giving children choices in your brochure for parents and in policy documents.

## Which One?

What can my body do?

### What are they learning?

are they
  using senses?
  making choices?
  trying new experiences?
  expressing likes and dislikes?
this leads to
  * using senses
  * making choices
  * describing

## Which One?

What can my body do?

**Walkers, talkers and pretenders**

**Aspect:**
A healthy child
**Components:**
making healthy choices

# All wrapped up –
twisting, folding, wrapping

## What you need
* old wallpaper, gift wrap and parcel wrap
* padded envelopes and small boxes
* short lengths of masking tape
* story books of different sizes

## What you do
1. Sit with the children and look through the paper and books.
2. Wrap up the books, tearing and folding the paper.
3. Help the children to choose books to wrap or put in the padded envelopes or boxes.
4. Talk about their choice of books. Try to use size words as well as talking about the pictures and stories.
5. When all the books are wrapped, stack them up and let each child in turn choose a book and then give it to another child to unwrap. Sit with the children and look through the paper and the books.

**another idea:**
* Have some noisy fun wrapping and unwrapping musical instruments.

## Ready for more?
- Use a marker pen to put a thick wavy line on large sheets of newspaper or old wallpaper. Practice tearing the paper along the line.
- Use small pieces of cellophane to wrap play dough.

## Individual needs

☼ Work together with children with fine motor difficulties, using larger, thicker sheets of paper.
☼ Use textured paper and a book with sounds or interesting textures for children with visual difficulties.
☼ Encourage children to use two hands together.

## Tiny Tip

✻ Pop bubble wrap for some great finger and thumb working together play.

## Watch, listen, reflect

👁 Watch to see how the children are manipulating the materials.
👁 Watch how they match up the size of the paper to the book to be wrapped.
👁 Listen for action and describing words used in short phrases.
👁 Are the children able to ask and respond to simple questions and comment on what they are doing?

## Working together

### Parents could:

* make some play dough for their child to play with at home.
* save gift-wrap, large envelopes and brown paper for you.

### Practitioners could:

* put together a fiddly bits box for exploring – full of clips, buttons, fasteners, tiny objects in boxes, rings, bits of elastic etc.
* encourage parents to make some play dough for the setting and also to sell to other parents as a fund-raiser.

## Which One?

What can my body do?

### What are they learning?

are they
   using two hands together?
   making choices?
   matching sizes?
   sharing?
   taking turns?
this leads to
   * hand control
   * using scissors
   * listening

## Which One?

What can my body do?

**Walkers, talkers and pretenders**

**Aspect:**
A healthy child
**Components:**
making healthy choices

# Baby time! –
baby play with everyday objects

## What you need

* a baby's feeding bottle, bottle brushes, bibs, small disposable nappies, potty, baby clothes
* baby toys such as a mobile, small rattles and baby books
* large baby dolls, dolls cot, high-chair or baby relaxer chair.

## What you do

1. Explore the objects together. Talk about the use of the objects and encourage the children to talk about babies in their families, babies they know and when they were babies.
2. Play alongside the children demonstrating object use and encouraging the children to use describing words, action words and words to describe feelings.
3. Model simple pretend play, talking or singing about what you are doing.

**another idea**:
* Make up some powdered milk together and pretend to feed the dolls.

## Ready for more?

- Make a baby clothes and equipment shop.
- Tear pictures of babies, baby equipment and toys from catalogues. Glue these in a scrapbook along with photos of the children when they were babies.

## Individual needs

☼ When helping children to imitate simple pretend play, such as feeding dolly, have two dolls and two spoons, one for you and one for the child.

☼ Make sure the clothes and feeding equipment are easy enough for small fingers or children with fine motor difficulties to manage.

## Tiny Tip

❉ Ask you health visitor if a group of children can visit a baby clinic to watch tiny babies being weighed.

## Watch, listen, reflect

👁 Listen for short phrases describing possession, such as baby's shoe, my brush and so on.

👁 Watch to see if children know what objects are used for as well as their names.

👁 Listen for children relating their play to their own experiences, such as 'This is just like my blanket when I was a baby'.

## Working together

### Parents could:

* try some simple pretend play at bath time, bathing dolly along with their child.
* bring in baby photos of their child, along with other suitable resources.

### Practitioners could:

* put up a list of baby related everyday objects needed, as well as a note about the importance of simple pretend play.
* learn some baby jingles and finger play rhymes to share with the children whilst playing alongside them.

## Which One?

What can my body do?

### What are they learning?

are they
 copying actions?
 pretending?
 sharing and turn taking?
 aware of the needs of others?
this leads to
 * helping others
 * making choices
 * social language

## Which One?

What can my body do?

**Walkers, talkers and pretenders**

**Aspect:**
A healthy child
**Components:**
making healthy choices

# Music makers –
### making choices with improvised instruments

## What you need
* three drawstring bags or pillow slips
* pan and wooden spoon
* small bag of rice
* washing up brush and colander

## What you do
1. Put the pan and wooden spoon in a bag, the rice in another and the brush and colander in the last bag.
2. Give the bags to the children to feel. Can they guess what is inside?
3. Take a look inside the bags and talk about the objects and their use. See if the children can tell you or show you what the objects are for.
4. See what different sounds you can make. Use describing words as well as action words to comment on what you hear and what the children are doing.
5. Pop all the instruments back in the bags, jumble the bags up and ask the children to try another bag.

**another idea:**
* Use Feely Bags to introduce new words and textures.

## Ready for more?
- Use the improvised instruments to tap out the rhythm of familiar songs.
- Go on a hunt together looking for objects that make different sounds.

## Individual needs

✿ For children that find holding a beater or stick difficult, fix short lengths of ribbon to beaters, so that they can fasten around wrists with Velcro.

✿ Look for beaters, sticks and instruments with easy to grip handles. Add non-slip tape or foam tubing to make grips wider.

## Tiny Tip

❋ Why not try music instruments outside – the noise can be easier to manage.

## Watch, listen, reflect

👁 Watch how children experiment with the improvised instruments.

👁 Listen to see if the children can hold a steady beat.

👁 Listen to the range of words and phrases they use to describe the sounds and actions they are making.

👁 Note how they are playing alongside each other, sharing and turn taking.

## Working together

### Parents could:

* play with their child making a pots and pans band!
* enjoy a range of music with their child, listening, singing and dancing together.

### Practitioners could:

* make sure the instruments are in good repair and stored where the children can get to them easily.
* establish some simple routines that allow all the children to have time enjoying the instruments, but avoid overwhelming noise!

## Which One?

What can my body do?

### What are they learning?

are they
  exploring?
  imitating?
  improvising?
  taking turns?
  making choices?
this leads to
  * rhythm
  * group work
  * following instructions

# Which One?

What can my body do?

**Walkers, talkers and pretenders**

**Aspect:**
A healthy child
**Components:**
making healthy choices

# Look at me! – exploring movement

## What you need
* a large space with a smooth clean floor
* bags of energy
* a chime bar, triangle or similar simple instrument

## What you do
1. Ask the children to lie down on the floor hugging their arms and knees ino their bodies. Strike the instrument and tell the children that this is their rest position.
2. When they hear the instrument again, they are to jump up and copy your actions. Try walking backwards, slithering along the floor, rolling, crawling and creeping along on tummies, forwards and backwards.
3. After a few moments of each activity, strike the instrument as a signal to return to the curled up rest position.
4. Make this fun by joining in and varying the length of time for each action, some very short and some much longer.

**another idea:**
* Play this game with children around the edge of a parachute.

## Ready for more?

- Hold a hoop up, or a length of ribbon with a partner, and encourage the children to crawl, roll, creep and slither under.
- Musical bumps, musical statues and traffic light games are all great for listening.

## Individual needs

☼ Think about the physical abilities of all the children and plan ahead the range of suggested movements.
☼ For children needing support with attention or listening skills, work with just two or three children in a group.
☼ Use bright yellow lines for VI children and use a plain surface in a well-lit area.

## Tiny Tip

✻ Finish lively games with a few moments quiet rest, perhaps lying on the floor listening to music.

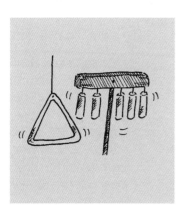

## Watch, listen, reflect

👁 Watch how the children focus and maintain their attention. Are they anticipating and listening for the chime bar signal.
👁 Listen to the range of language the children are using. Are they using position words, such as under, high, low, near, far?
👁 Look at how they are relating to and imitating each other.

## Working together

### Parents could:

* dance with their child at home.
* visit the park and other open spaces, and play follow my leader to help their child try different ways of moving.

### Practitioners could:

* look at the range of opportunities for physical play, and plan how these can be developed.
* talk to parents about each child's developing physical skills, and how the setting is encouraging them.

## Which One?

What can my body do?

### What are they learning?

are they
   aware of personal space?
   imitating actions?
   listening and attending?
this leads to
   * confidence
   * simple rules
   * changing direction

## Which One?

What can my body do?

**Walkers, talkers and pretenders**

**Aspect:**
A healthy child
**Components:**
making healthy choices

# Special - it's mine! - comforters and special toys

## What you need
* the children's comfort or special toys, favourite teddy bears, etc.

## What you do
1. Hold the first toy or blanket carefully and explain how important this is to the child, and that we must take very good care of it. Hand it to the child it belongs to.
2. Invite the children to tell you about their comfort toys. Try to use words to describe feelings.
3. Next, explain that you have a new song all about favourite toys, teddies and blankets. Encourage the children to hold their comfort toys and join in with the rhyme, using the tune of 'Twinkle, Twinkle Little Star'.

   *Gently, gently special toy, how I love you, love you so,
   You're so special all for me, like a warm hug near to me,
   Gently, gently now you know, how I love you, love you so.*
   Sing the song again as you hold and hug the comforters.

## Ready for more?
- Introduce the children to your childhood special toy, or a toy belonging to your family.
- Decorate shoeboxes to make a special place for each child to keep their comfort toy, at home, or at the setting.

## Individual needs

☼ Make a special safe place for children to leave comfort toys that they need to bring to your group. Make this easily accessible, but reassure them that other children cannot play with their comfort object unless they say they can.

☼ Use simple language and short phrases for children with communication difficulties.

## Tiny Tip

❈ Looking at comfort toys is a great way to develop a circle time routine.

## Watch, listen, reflect

◉ Watch to see if children recognise the tune and can start to join in with the new words.

◉ Listen to the language they use to describe their comforters. Are they able to maintain attention when other children are speaking?

◉ Think about how aware children are of the needs of the others. How do they show this?

## Working together

### Parents could:

* reassure their child that they can bring their comfort toy to the group, if needed.
* establish a sensitive but consistent bedtime routine, including comfort toys.

### Practitioners could:

* talk to parents about comfort toys and their importance to their child's emotional development.
* make sure new parents are reassured about the respect and care that will be given to their child's special toy or object.

## Which One?

What can my body do?

### What are they learning?

are they
  aware of their own needs?
  aware of the needs of others?
  enjoying new songs?
this leads to
  * group awareness
  * making choices
  * listening

# Which One?

**What can my body do?**

**Walkers, talkers and pretenders**

**Aspect:**
A healthy child
**Components:**
making healthy choices

# I like ...... - choosing favourites

## What you need

* pieces of fabric and clothes with different patterns and textures - stripes and spots, plain colours, different textures, woolly hats, net curtains, rubber gloves, etc.
* washing basket, plastic crate, pegs, washing line

## What you do

1. Rummage through the fabrics together, talking about the colours, patterns, and feel of the different fabrics.
2. Encourage the children to talk about things they have at home that are the same colour, or have similar patterns.
3. Take turns to choose a favourite item and peg it on the washing line.
4. Look at each piece as it hangs on the line, talking about patterns, textures, colours and favourites.

**another idea:**
* Sort the washing into piles, all the red things together, all the stripes, and so on.

## Ready for more?

- Take turns to find clothes by their colour and size. Peg these on the line – can you find something big and blue?
- Have a real washday outside with lots of soapy water, bubbles and pegs!

## Individual needs

✿ Make sure the washing line is at a height that less mobile children can also reach. Some children just starting to stand independently may need to be supported in standing, or seated.
✿ Make sure the line is positioned where the most active children won't run into it.

## Tiny Tip

❋ Children love to peg up aprons on a line – a really easy way to clear the soggy heap of aprons lurking under the water tray!

## Watch, listen, reflect

◉ Watch to see how children use two hands together to peg the washing on the line.
◉ Look to see how they resolve problems they encounter, such as holding the pegs and stretching the item onto the line at the same time.
◉ Listen to the language they use to describe the items.

## Working together

### Parents could:

* bring in suitable items for the activity
* set up a simple clothesline for their child to peg up socks on.

### Practitioners could:

* talk to parents about how this activity helps their child to use two hands together as well as mathematical words such as shape, colour and size.
* add a simple clothesline and peg basket to the home corner and the toy library.

## Which One?

What can my body do?

### What are they learning?

are they
 using two hands?
 exploring?
 responding?
 making choices?
this leads to
 * hand control
 * making choices
 * maths language
 * describing

# Which One?

What can my body do?

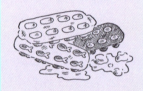

**Aspect:**
A healthy child
**Components:**
keeping safe

# Resources

## Things to collect

Pictures from magazines and catalogues for discussion
Baby clothes to use with big dolls
Baby items such as bottles, small disposable nappies, clothes, hats, etc
Fabrics for parachute games and swinging
Night and day clothes for teddies and dolls
Small beds and cots (or boxes) and bedclothes
Torches and battery lights
Fabrics to make tents and shelters
Natural and everyday objects for treasure and exploration baskets
Shallow baskets and trays
Small empty containers, ice cube trays, small yogurt pots etc.
Hats, scarves and gloves of all types, sizes and materials
Spoons of all sizes
Wallpaper, wrapping paper, tissue, masking tape

## For cooking and making food (real and pretend)

* plastic plates and beakers (IKEA has a good value selection)
* small plastic jugs (check that they pour well)
* spoons for serving (look for ones with chunky handles)
* small knives for cutting fruit, bread, etc (butter knives are good)
* plastic or fabric tablecloths

# Books and Stories

**The Little Book of Parachute Play** by Clare Beswick; Featherstone Education

**Be Safe** - The Association for Science Education from www.ase.org.uk (Safety advice for nursery and primary schools and settings)

**Road Safety Guidance** (from your local authority)

**This Little Puffin** has a whole section of baby songs and rhymes

**Collect some books about childhood fears and anxieties**, and add some which emphasise security and safety.
  * Fact books and stories about first experiences of visiting the dentist, the doctor, being in hospital, having a new baby, going away to stay etc.
  * Books about visits and family experiences, including celebrations, happy events, parties etc.
  * Books about families and feeling safe, bedtime and being looked after.
  * Stories about night time, monsters, dinosaurs and other frightening experiences, so children can 'practice being scared' in a safe environment.

You could ask your local librarian for suggestions of new and well loved titles - they may be prepared to lend some to your setting.

## Which One?

What can my body do?

**Aspect:**
A healthy child
**Components:**
keeping safe

# The Little Baby Book Series

The structure of the series has been developed to support the Birth to Three Matters Guidance, issued in 2003 by the DfES/SureStart. The series is structured to follow the aspects contained within the guidance:

**Purple Books support the development of a Strong Child:**
a child who is secure, confident and aware of him\herself, feeling a valued and important member of their family, their group and their setting.

**Pink Books support the development of a Skilful Communicator:**
a child who is sociable, good at communicating with adults and other children, listens and communicates with confidence, who enjoys and plays with words in discussion, stories, songs and rhymes.

**Green Books support the development of a Competent Learner:**
a child who uses play to explore and make sense of their world, creating, imagining, and representing their experiences.

**Blue Books support the development of a Healthy Child:**
a child who is well nourished and well supported, feels safe and protected, and uses that sense of security to grow, both physically and emotionally, becoming independent and able to make choices in their play and learning.

The First Four books (Published in April 2003) are:
*What I Really Want* (Purple Books)
*I Like You, You Like Me* (Pink Books)
*Touch it Feel it* (Green Books)
*Grab and Let Go* (Blue Books)

The next four books (also containing one book from each aspect) are published in October 2003.

©Featherstone Education Ltd, 2004
Text © Sally Featherstone, Clare Beswick, 2004
Illustrations © Martha Hardy, 2004
Series Editor, Sally Featherstone

First published in the UK, June 2004

*The right of Sally Featherstone and Clare Beswick to be identified as authors of this work has been asserted in accordance with Sections 77 and 78 of the Copyright, Designs and Patents Act, 1988.*

*All rights reserved. No part of this publication may be reproduced by any means, stored in a retrieval system, or transmitted in any form or by any means, electronic, mechanical, photocopying, recording or otherwise, without the prior written consent of the publisher. This book may not be lent, sold, hired out or otherwise disposed of by way of trade in any form of binding or with any cover other than that in which it is published without the prior consent of the publisher, and without this condition being imposed upon the subsequent user.*

Published in the United Kingdom by
Featherstone Education Ltd
44 - 46 High Street
Husbands Bosworth
Leicestershire
LE17 6LP

Would you like to be on our mailing list to receive information about our other products and publications for the under 5s? If so please email your contact details to info@featherstone.uk.com. We will from time to time send you our catalogue and leaflets through the post. We will not telephone you. We will not pass your details to any other company.